Steck-Vaughn Shutterbug Books SCIENCE

Stormy Weather

by Ellen Catala

STECK-VAUGHN

Harcourt Supplemental Publishers

www.steck-vaughn.com

Dark clouds gather overhead.

CRASH!

You see lightning flash in the sky.

BOOM!

You hear the crack of thunder.

Rain pours down.

It's a **thunderstorm!**

4

Thunderclouds are made of many tiny drops of water.
The tiny drops are called droplets.
The droplets come together and form larger drops.
During a thunderstorm, these large drops fall as rain.
The crashing water droplets also make electricity.
The electricity turns into a flash of lightning and a
boom of thunder.

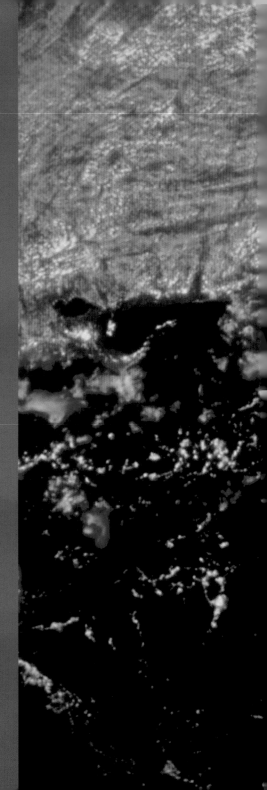

Sometimes large storms form over the ocean.

The air in the storm begins to swirl around.

The air moves faster and faster.

More and more air is sucked into the twirling clouds.

A **hurricane** has begun!

A hurricane may pass over land.
The storm brings very heavy rain and strong wind.
The wind can pull up trees and knock down houses.
It can even pick up boats from the ocean and drop them on land.

A **tornado** is smaller than a hurricane.
But tornadoes are also very powerful.
Warm, wet air is pulled up into a thundercloud.
The air swirls around at high speeds.
Suddenly, a funnel-shaped cloud forms.
When a tornado touches the ground, it can
destroy almost anything in its path.

Sometimes the air inside a cloud is very cold.

The droplets of water form ice crystals.

Ice crystals come together to form snowflakes.

The snowflakes fall as snow.

A large amount of snow and strong winds together make a **blizzard**.

Even the biggest storms will end.

Wait inside until the storm is over.

Soon the dark clouds will disappear.

The sun will shine again.

Then, if you're lucky, you might see a rainbow!

Stormy Weather

Thunderstorm

Hurricane

Tornado

Blizzard